Entrepreneurial Wit & Wisdom

A book for managers who want to manage as entrepreneurs. It represents the thoughts and actions of some of this country's most successful managers and entrepreneurs and their ideas of how to practice entrepreneurial behavior within the corporate structure.

ACKNOWLEDGEMENTS

While I have taken a number of years to synthesize the ideas in this book, they would never have gotten in the stage to be published without the help of friends, associates, and practicing entrepreneurs. They are:

Dick Bagwell, *President of Bagwell & Associates*

Robert A. Beck, *Chairman & CEO of the Prudential Insurance Company and 1985 Chairman of the Prestigious Business Roundtable*

Len Berry, *Professor of Marketing, Texas A&M University, and President of the American Marketing Association*

Roland S. Boreham, Jr., *Chairman & CEO, Baldor Electric Company*

Mickey Cissell, *President & CEO of Sunbelt Courier*

Governor Bill Clinton, *State of Arkansas*

Bill Cravens, *Chairman & CEO of Worthen Banking Corporation*

Jim Donnelly, *Professor of Marketing, University of Kentucky*

Peter F. Drucker

Bill Fackler, *Executive Vice President, Barnett Banks of Florida*

Jeff Farris, *President, University of Central Arkansas*

Roberto Goizueta, *Chairman & CEO, The Coca-Cola Company*

Lee Griffin, *President & CEO, Louisiana National Bank*

Dan Horton, *CEO of Horton & Associates, Inc.*

Max E. Link, *President & CEO of Sandoz, Inc.*

Tom McRae, *President, The Winthrop Rockefeller Foundation*

Don Mosley, *Professor of Management & Former Dean of Business, University of South Alabama*

Bill Patterson, *Vice President, University of Central Arkansas*

John E. Robson, *Chief Operating Officer, G. D. Searle*

Clara Jones Rowntree, *Owner, Jones Oil Company*

William Smithberg, *Chairman & CEO, Quaker Oats Company*

Dick Snelsire, *Group Vice President, Wachovia Bank*

William Sommers, *Executive Vice President, Booz, Allen & Hamilton Inc.*

Jack Stephens, *Chairman of Stephens Inc.*

John E. Swearingen, *Chairman & CEO of Continental Banking Corporation and retired Chairman & CEO of Standard Oil of Indiana*

Helen Walton, *Honorary Chairman, Board of Trustees, The College of the Ozarks*

Jack Whittle, *Chairman & CEO of Whittle and Hanks*

Special acknowledgements to Mickey Freeman, Dianne Newcity and Linda Marshall. Mickey for his gift of creative criticism and constant encouragement and Dianne and Linda for their expert typing and eagle-eyed proofing.

Needless to say, all the fuzzy thinking, faulty logic, oversights and just plain mistakes are my fault.

FOREWORD

When we examine what has been happening in our economy over the last few years, we see a lot of things to be happy about. One of the things that has pleased me most has been the re-emergence of the entrepreneur. This re-emergence has taken place not only in the traditional sense of the risk-taking owner, but also by more and more individuals practicing entrepreneurial behavior throughout the organization. These entrepreneurs are always looking for opportunities where perhaps others do not. In every success and every failure they are trying to understand what really happened, so they can find a way to use the successes and failures to their advantage.

I think Dr. Qualls' book is a clever way of communicating the entrepreneurial philosophy. It should be most helpful to those who are current practitioners as well as those that want to learn a little more about it. Don't be lead astray by the apparent simplicity of the concepts in this book, because they represent the thoughts and actions of some of this country's most successful managers and entrepreneurs.

At Wal-Mart our Associates have demonstrated over and over again that entrepreneurship is contagious and I recommend it to you.

Sam M. Walton

Sam M. Walton
Chairman & CEO
Wal-Mart

PART ONE

Philosophy
Commitment
Innovation

If you can't find a way,
make one.

*Don't spend your time
stomping out ants when
elephants are coming over
the wall.*

RULE 3:

Remember, if you are not the lead dog the scene never changes.

RULE 4:

In order to catch a fast horse, you must ride a fast horse.

RULE 5:

Don't think you hit a triple if you were born on third base.

RULE 6:

Become a monomaniac with a mission.

RULE 7:

Success comes to him who waits if he works like hell while he waits.

RULE 8:

Even if you are on the right track, you'll get run over if you just sit there.

RULE 9:

Occasionally in error, but never in doubt.

PART TWO

Decision Making
Leadership
Motivation

If you're not falling down, you're not learning.

RULE 11:

It's easier to ask forgiveness than permission.

*Instill in your managers
a sense of urgency when
there is no emergency.*

RULE 13:

Fatigue makes cowards of us all.

RULE 14:

Total company involvement is the name of the game.

You can observe a lot by just looking.

DIZZY DEAN, FORMER BASEBALL GREAT, WAS
FOND OF SAYING THIS AND IT IS A CARDINAL RULE
FOR THE ENTREPRENEUR.

RULE 16:

Practice one part listening
for every part speaking.

RULE 17:

Don't get tangled in your own underwear.

Often a bad decision is better than no decision at all.

RULE 19:

Become as concerned about the sins of omission as the sins of commission.

When you fire someone, get them off the property before they tear something up.

AN OLD RULE OF THE RAILROAD
THAT STILL HAS APPLICATION TODAY.

PART THREE
Risks
Rewards
Profits

If you want to walk on water, you have got to get out of the boat.

RULE 22:

Buy low and sell high.

RULE 23:

Know when to hold them and know when to fold them.

Don't talk about revenue enhancement when the name of the game is "getting the order."

NYSE COMPANY CHAIRMAN AND CEO, R.S. BOREHAM SAYS THAT MAKING THE SALE IS AT THE HEART OF THE ENTREPRENEURS THINKING, WHILE THE RATIONALIST FOCUSES ON ANALYTICAL CONCEPTS.

RULE 25:

Don't confuse brains with a bull market.

RULE 26:

Sure the bottom line is important, but don't forget the top line.

Never turn down a good deal because of the lack of money.

Jack Stephens, Chairman of Stephens Inc., largest "Wall Street" firm off Wall Street, says, "If a deal is a good deal, you can always find ways to finance it."

PART FOUR

Planning
Marketing
Selling

RULE 28:

Remember, there is always an easy solution to every human problem—neat, plausible, and wrong.

RULE 29:

Those that make the plans must implement them.

RULE 30:

*Get the herd headed
roughly west.*

Become a niche picker.

PACO'S
MEX-TEX
FOOD

HOT TAMALES   CHILI CON CARNI
TACOS   NACHOS
BURRITOES   ENCHILADAS

ABE'S
STOMACH
REMEDIES

ALKA-SEL
MALANTA
TUMS

DON GUIDO'S
Spicy
ITALIAN FOOD

Get the facts, there has to be a way.

RULE 33:

Don't spend your time trying to do well something you should not have been doing at all.

What is perceived is real.

RULE 35:

*Guard against diversifications
becoming diversions.*

You can only sell John Smith what John Smith buys, when you sell John Smith through John Smith's eyes.

RULE 37:

Don't subscribe to the "lose bucks on every individual sale, but make it up in volume" theory.

PART FIVE

The Entrepreneur

Don't take yourself too seriously.

NOTES: This rulebook draws mostly from personal conversations secondary sources and correspondence with various individuals. As nearly as possible, credit for the idea or thought is given, but in some cases, it is impossible to give credit since a number of ideas and thoughts are synthesized into a single rule.

Rule 1: Permission obtained from Robert A. Beck, Chairman & CEO of the Prudential Insurance Company and 1985 Chairman of the Prestigious Business Roundtable.

Rule 2: Permission obtained from Jack Whittle, Chairman & CEO, Whittle and Hanks, a premier bank consulting firm.

Rule 3: Permission obtained from Ward Ramsay who acquainted me with this axiom.

Rule 4: Mochtar Riady, head of the Lippo Group, is fond of quoting this old Chinese proverb.

Rule 6: Permission obtained from Peter F. Drucker.

Rule 8: Will Rogers.

Rule 10: Permission obtained from William Smithburg, Chairman & CEO, Quaker Oats Company.

Rule 12: Permission obtained from William Sommers, Executive Vice President, Booz, Allen & Hamilton Inc. This statement was made with respect to John F. Welch, Jr., Chairman & CEO of General Electric Company, desire to upgrade GE's performance in each of its major markets to the "No. 1 or No. 2 position."

Rule 13: The late great Vince Lombardi.

Rule 14: Permission obtained from Sam Walton, Chairman, CEO and Founder of Wal-Mart, who shared these feelings with me about the success of Wal-Mart.

Rule 16: Permission obtained from Max E. Link, President & CEO of Sandoz, Inc.

Rule 17: Permission obtained from John E. Robson, Chief Operating Officer, G. D. Searle.

Rule 18: Permission obtained from Lee Griffin, President & CEO of Louisiana National Bank and a friend, going back to our graduate school days.

Rule 20: Permission obtained from Mickey Cissell, President of Sunbelt Courier, who first introduced me to this axiom.

Rule 21: Permission obtained from Fritz Ehren, President, The College of the Ozarks.

Rule 22: Has been said by many at different times and places, but I have always enjoyed the way it was first told to me. As the story goes, Archibald MacLeish was lecturing to his class at Harvard and one of his students said, "Professor, we are all graduating seniors, would you give us some good advice?" MacLeish thought a moment and said, "Buy low and sell high."

Rule 23: From Kenny Rogers' hit record, "The Gambler." Permission obtained by Writers Night Music, P.O. Box 22635, Nashville, TN 37202.

Rule 26: Permission obtained from Roland S. Boreham, Jr., Chairman & CEO of Baldor Electric Company.

Rule 27: Permission obtained from Jack Stephens, Chairman of Stephens Inc., largest "Wall Street" firm off Wall Street, who shared this thought with me. He said, "If a deal is a *good* deal, you can always find ways to finance it."

Rule 28: H. L. Mencken.

Rule 29: The late Patrick Haggerty, long-time Chairman & CEO of Texas Instruments.

Rule 32: Permission obtained from Bill Cravens, Chairman & CEO of Worthen Banking Corporation, who says and practices this axiom.

Rule 33: Permission obtained from Roberto Goizueta, Chairman & CEO, The Coca-Cola Company.

Rule 34: Permission obtained from Patricia Phillips, Worthen Bank & Trust Company, N.A., who passed this axiom along.

Rule 35: Permission obtained from John E. Swearingen, Chairman & CEO, Continental Banking Corporation, Chicago, and retired Chairman & CEO of Standard Oil of Indiana.

Rule 37: Permission obtained from Jack Whittle, Chairman & CEO of Whittle and Hanks.

About The Authors

Robert L. Qualls is Executive Vice President of Finance for Baldor Electric Company. He previously served in various capacities at Worthen Banking Corporation, including Chairman and CEO of an affiliate bank and Executive Vice President of the lead bank. He was also a cabinet officer in the administration of Governor Bill Clinton and President of the College of the Ozarks. Dr. Qualls is the author of a number of articles and co-author of a book published by Trinity University Press (1979) and a chapter in the book *Management Techniques For Specialized Institutions* by Jossey-Bass (1983).

Sherrie Shepherd began cartooning as a hobby to entertain herself and her family. She received a B.A. in Art from the University of Arkansas at Little Rock, emphasizing her studies in the area of graphic art. Formerly employed as an artist in the Marketing Department of Worthen Bank and Trust Company, N.A., she now works as a freelance artist, and is under contract with United Feature Syndicate. The cartoon strip she does for United Feature appears in newspapers across the country under the title of "Francie." In Arkansas the strip is carried by the *Arkansas Democrat.* Her cartoons have appeared in *Complete Woman, Medical Economics, Woman, Ebony* and *Cosmopolitan* magazines.